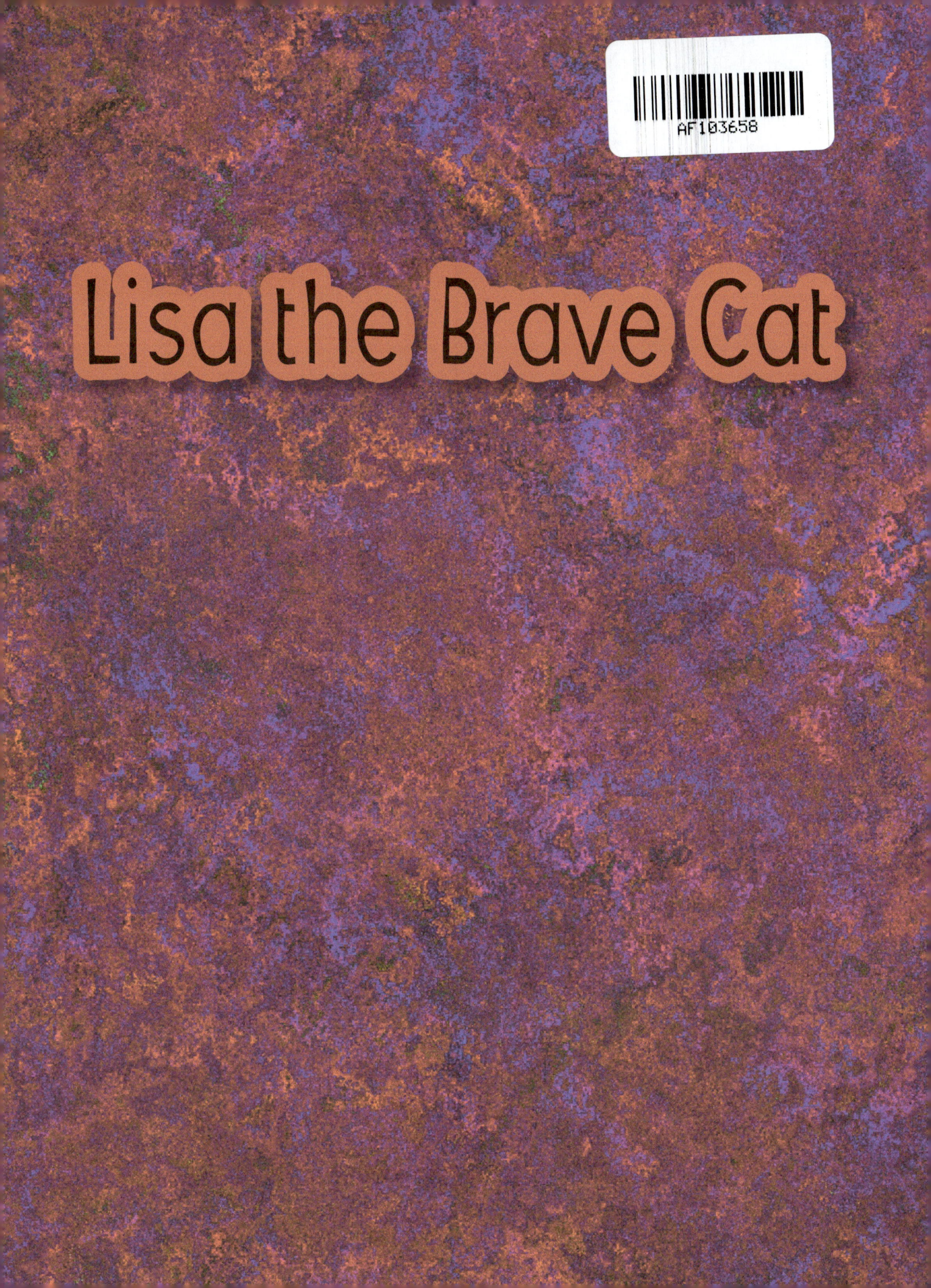
Lisa the Brave Cat

Lisa The Brave Cat

Published by Gatekeeper Press
3971 Hoover Rd. Suite 77
Columbus, OH 43123-2839
www.GatekeeperPress.com

Copyright © 2017 by Aleksandra Saransky
Photographs by Olena Sharapova
Copyrights by Aleksandra Charapova

All rights reserved. Neither this book, nor any parts within it may be sold or reproduced in any form or by any electronic or mechanical means, including information storage and retrieval systems without permission in writing from the author. The only exception is by a reviewer, who may quote short excerpts in a review.

ISBN: 9781619848344
eISBN: 9781619848351

Printed in the United States of America

Lisa the Brave Cat

Aleksandra Saransky

gatekeeper press
Columbus, Ohio

LISA WAS A BEAUTIFUL, FURRY WHITE PERSIAN CAT. SHE LIVED IN A NICE HOUSE WITH A HUGE BACKYARD. THE YARD HAD A POOL AND A GARDEN. SHE CONSIDERED THE BACKYARD TO BE HER PROPERTY, AND SHE TOOK CARE OF IT WITH GREAT RESPONSIBILITY. THE HOUSE WAS THE PROPERTY OF HER MASTERS, BUT LISA WAS THE QUEEN OF THE HOUSE, BACKYARD, AND GARDEN.

IN THE MORNING, LISA LIKED TO SIT ON THE PORCH AND WATCH THE BIRDS FLY BY, OR SIT IN THE TREE'S BRANCHES.

IN THE DAYTIME, SHE USUALLY SLEPT SOMEWHERE IN THE HOUSE. SHE HAD HER OWN HIDING PLACES, WHERE NOBODY COULD FIND HER AND BOTHER HER WHILE SHE WAS NAPPING.

BUT THE FUN TIME FOR LISA WAS IN THE EVENING. SHE WOULD WAIT PATIENTLY FOR HER MASTER TO COME HOME FROM WORK. USUALLY, HE WOULD PUT HER ON HIS SHOULDER (HE WAS VERY TALL). AND THEN, THEY WOULD WALK AROUND THE PROPERTY. LISA WAS SO HIGH, THAT SHE COULD OBSERVE EVERYTHING. SHE WAS VERY PROUD OF HERSELF AND WAS SURE, THAT EVERYBODY WAS WATCHING HER WITH JEALOUSY, EVEN THE NEIGHBOR'S CAT.

THE NEIGHBOR'S CAT WAS NEVER THAT HIGH. SHE COULD SEE ALL THE ANTS, BUGS, AND BUTTERFLIES IN THE FLOWER BEDS, AND SHE KNEW THAT THEY WERE JEALOUS, TOO.

BUT ONE DAY SOMETHING EXTRAORDINARY HAPPENED. THEY WERE WALKING AROUND THE BACKYARD AS USUAL, CHECKING UP ON EVERYTHING, WHEN LISA SAW SOMETHING MOVING IN THE GRASS, NEAR THE FLOWER BED. OH YES, SHE COULD SEE IT NOW... IT WAS A SNAKE!

LISA KNEW THAT SHE HAD TO WARN HER MASTER, AND SHE LET OUT A LOUD THREATENING "MEOW" SOUND, AS IF SHE WERE READY FOR ATTACK.

THE MASTER WAS SURPRISED. HE KNEW THAT LISA WAS TRYING TO WARN HIM ABOUT SOMETHING. HE TURNED HIS HEAD AND ASKED, "WHAT IS IT, LISA?" THEN, HE SAW THE SNAKE, TOO. "LISA, DON'T MOVE, LET'S GET OUT OF HERE QUIETLY," HE SAID.

BUT LISA WAS READY TO JUMP DOWN AND FIGHT WITH THE SNAKE. SHE WANTED TO PROTECT HER MASTER AND HER PROPERTY. BUT THE MASTER HELD HER TIGHTLY AND SAID AGAIN: "LET'S JUST GO AWAY. THE SNAKE IS NOT GOING TO HURT US."

AND INDEED, THE SNAKE DECIDED TO DO THE SAME THING. SHE STARTED CRAWLING AWAY, AND IN A SECOND, SHE JUST DISAPPEARED.

"HOORAY!" THOUGHT LISA, "GO AWAY, AND DON'T COME BACK!" SHE WAS SO PROUD OF HERSELF. SHE HAD WARNED HER MASTER AND SCARED THE SNAKE AWAY.

THE MASTER PETTED LISA AND SAID, "GOOD JOB, LISA. I HOPE,

THE SNAKE WILL NOT COME BACK ANYMORE," AND THEY WALKED BACK
TOWARDS THE HOUSE.

WHEN THE SUN SET AND DARKNESS SURROUNDED THE BACKYARD, EVERYTHING BECAME MYSTERIOUS. LISA WAS LYING DOWN ON THE PORCH, WATCHING THE LIGHTNING BUGS AND LISTENING TO THE SOUNDS OF THE NIGHT. THAT WAS REALLY HER FAVORITE TIME. AFTER ALL, SHE WAS A NIGHT CREATURE.

"GOOD LUCK WITH YOUR HUNTING, LISA!" SAID THE MASTER, AND HE WENT INSIDE.

LISA KNEW THAT SOON SHE WOULD HAVE TO GO IN, TOO. BUT SHE ALSO KNEW THAT SHE HAD A LOT OF MICE – TOYS – THAT SHE WAS GOING TO PLAY WITH ALL NIGHT.

NOT EVERYBODY COULD BELIEVE THIS, BUT LISA ALSO HAD HER OWN IPAD, WITH HER FAVORITE GAME, "CATCH THE MOUSE." SHE COULD PLAY FOR HOURS WITH IT.

LISA CURLED UP, CLOSED HER EYES, AND STARTED DREAMING ABOUT HER MASTER AND THE FUN SHE WAS GOING TO HAVE TONIGHT AND TOMORROW.

www.ingramcontent.com/pod-product-compliance
Lightning Source LLC
LaVergne TN
LVHW072114060526
838200LV00061B/4894